101 WAYS TO SECRETLY RUIN YOUR COWORKER'S DAY

Tons of Office Pranks, Endless Laughs,

Sneaky Tricks, and So Much More!

JACK HAYNES

ISBN: 978-1-957590-49-3

For questions, email: Support@AwesomeReads.org

Please consider writing a review!

Just visit: AwesomeReads.org/review

FREE BONUS

SCAN TO GET OUR NEXT BOOK FOR FREE!

Table of Contents

INTRODUCTION

Welcome to *101 Ways to Secretly Ruin Your Coworker's Day*, the ultimate gag gift to help you add some mischief to your office routines. This book contains a mix of silly jokes to make your coworkers laugh or get revenge on a fellow prankster. Some are simple enough to carry out with just a few office supplies, while others will require a bit of an investment.

Before you get started, you'll probably want to work on your sneaking skills and practice keeping a straight face. It's also a good idea to check your office's policies and make sure you understand the culture at work. The last thing you want is to go overboard and end up in trouble with human resources, or worse, the police.

The goal should be to stir up some chaos without hurting anyone or disrupting important tasks. Each chapter contains a list of pranks with a common theme. You can either complete them all in a row or jump around to keep your coworkers guessing.

It's up to you to decide whether or not to take credit for your shenanigans. Sometimes, it's more fun when your coworkers are actively searching for the prankster in the office. If they don't catch you right away, it'll become an office mystery. Complaining about pranks can throw people off your trail.

However, it's unlikely that you'll remain incognito forever. Once people know you're the office joker, you should expect to have a few pranks pulled on you in return. You might even start a trend throughout the entire company.

The important thing is to be respectful. Choose your audience carefully, and don't hesitate to apologize if one of your jokes doesn't quite land. Fortunately, this book contains many different pranks for you to choose from, ranging from harmless to a bit risqué. Good luck, and have fun!

CHAPTER ONE:

DESK DALLIANCES

Most people have a designated area at work, even if they don't have a separate office. It's common for employees to add personal effects like knickknacks or family photos to make their areas feel cozier. While these details are a great way to get to know your coworkers, they're also clues about what will get under their skin.

Messing with a coworker's desk is a classic way to get a laugh. Keeping your tricks limited to one person's desk also makes it easier to target a specific coworker. This way, you can prank someone with a similar sense of humor who will view your pranks as intended. Otherwise, you could accidentally end up disturbing coworkers you don't know well or interrupt an important project.

This chapter includes ideas to help you mess with your coworkers while they're away. Between lunchtime and bathroom breaks, you should have plenty of opportunities to sneak in and cause a little chaos. Just remember not to cause any permanent damage to office equipment or personal belongings.

[1]
SWITCHING
DESKS

Switching a coworker's desk with someone else's is bound to cause confusion. This trick is particularly effective if you switch two desks that are already close together. If your coworker isn't paying attention, they might just look for their decorations and walk to their desk without realizing it's in a slightly different spot.

Depending on the layout of your office, you might be able to prank two people at once by switching their desks when they're both away. Ask another coworker to help if you won't have enough time to shuffle everything by yourself. Your coworkers will return to their cubicles only to find another person's belongings. Depending on how gullible they are, you might be able to convince them that your boss wanted the department to reorganize the area.

[2]
MOUSE
MAYHEM

No one likes computer trouble, and some people are more tech savvy than others. You don't need to make a huge change to get a funny reaction from your coworker. Something as simple as changing the sensitivity of their mouse could be enough to drive them up a wall. A slow mouse is aggravating to move around, while a jumpy one makes it impossible to click on the right objects.

Of course, you'll need access to their computer to change the sensitivity. If their computer is always locked, try sticking some double-sided tape on the bottom of their mouse instead. They won't be able to use their mouse, and they'll waste time troubleshooting the problem. This low-tech alternative is still amusing, even if it doesn't quite have the same effect.

[3]
STICKY
SITUATIONS

The first step of this prank is to get a pack of sticky notes. While most offices have them on hand, it's better to purchase your own if you think you might get in trouble for wasting supplies. Next, cover your coworker's desk or cubicle in sticky notes. For the biggest visual impact, put sticky notes on every surface, including the floor and the sides of their cubicle.

If you have time, incorporate different colors to make objects stand out. Use yellow on their computer and pink on their chair. You can also draw funny pictures on the sticky notes, leave a message, or create a design like a smiley face.

Don't forget about the windows. Ideally, your coworker will be able to see the sticky notes from the parking lot and know that their office has been pranked. It'll be a long walk heading inside to see how much chaos awaits them.

[4]
SMALL
CHANGES

Most people will instantly catch on if you move their furniture or belongings some distance away, but they may not be observant enough to notice small changes over time. For instance, you could move a coworker's desk an inch per day or slowly nudge their filing cabinet out of arm's reach. See how long it takes them to realize they're sitting in a new spot or reaching farther to get a file out of the cabinet.

This strategy works better if your office has dense carpet that won't leave imprints from furniture. If moving a large item would be too obvious, shuffling around office supplies or gradually relocating a lamp can work, too. Once it's become undeniable that someone is moving your coworker's stuff around, you can come clean for a good laugh and reveal how long it's taken them to figure it out.

[5]
EYES UP

Googly eyes add a bit of humor to even the most mundane objects. They're portable enough to keep in your pocket while you wait for the perfect opportunity to arise. Plus, they're easy to stick on and remove without any hassle.

This type of harmless joke is great for coworkers who enjoy a laugh but wouldn't welcome a more involved prank that takes over their entire desk. Be careful about putting googly eyes on family photos, unless you know more about the people involved. For example, you don't want to accidentally put googly eyes on a loved one who's passed away.

In addition to putting googly eyes on your coworkers' belongings, it could also be fun to target communal areas like the break room. Imagine grabbing a cup of coffee, only to discover that all the sugar packets have eyes! Your peers may even join in and relocate googly eyes to other places you don't expect.

[6]
UPS AND DOWNS

In busy offices, it's tough to find enough time to play a practical joke without someone seeing you. Adjusting your coworker's armrest or moving their seat down is a quick prank that only takes a few seconds. You can dart into their area, change their chair, and be back at your own desk in under a minute.

Choose your targets with care. If you know someone uses their armrests for support, or they're a little unsteady on their feet, adjusting their chair could cause an injury. The same applies if you reach in and lower someone's chair while they're sitting in it.

[7]
UNPLUGGED ANARCHY

Another quick prank is to unplug your coworker's keyboard or mouse. Make sure to hide the end of the wire in such a way that it still looks plugged in. If they use wireless versions, you'll need to remove the receiver from the USB port.

Most people will attempt to work through the issue on their computer before checking the hardware. They may even ask you for advice when they can't get it to work. For an extra challenge, hide the wireless receiver somewhere in their cubicle and leave your coworker clues as to where to find it.

[8]
PACKED UP

Since this prank takes time and involves moving around a lot of material, you might want to wait until your coworker goes home for the day. Once they're gone, find an unlocked drawer or receptacle to fill up with packing material. When they go to grab a file or get a stapler out of their desk, they'll find a surprise instead.

Make sure to choose a basic filler, such as packing peanuts or shredded paper. If you know your coworker is celebrating a personal milestone or event, you can even fill their drawers with confetti. Avoid using edible items, like popcorn, which could attract pests. The joke will be on *you* if you fill your coworker's desk with food and come back to an infestation.

To make this joke more annoying, hide their trash can in another part of the building. They'll go to clean out their drawer and realize they're missing the wastebasket. They'll either need to borrow someone else's, find their own, or get a trash bag from the supply closet.

[9]
THAT'S
A WRAP

Have you ever heard of people encasing their friends' cars in plastic wrap or covering their couches in tinfoil? This idea translates to the office, too. You can decide whether you want to wrap individual items or just focus on large surfaces. Plastic wrap from your kitchen will be fine for smaller pranks, but you could also consider getting large rolls of plastic from the hardware store.

Another fun variation is to wrap your coworker's desk for a miniature party. If you know their birthday, you can use wrapping paper with a cake and candles. For the holidays, choose paper with snowmen, reindeer, or other festive themes.

However, keep in mind that this can be a time-consuming prank to clean up. If you know a coworker has a time-sensitive task or a critical meeting coming up, it's probably wise to delay your schemes. You don't want to upset them or jeopardize their progress on a project by making them waste an hour unwrapping their possessions.

[10]
YOU CALLED?

The next time you know two coworkers will be away from their desks at the same time, leave them each a note from the other person asking for a phone call. A handwritten note seems more urgent than a virtual request, so they'll be more likely to call right away.

This prank is even more enjoyable if you can lurk nearby and eavesdrop on the conversation. You'll get to listen to them try to figure out what caused the miscommunication, as both of them deny leaving a note in the first place.

CHAPTER TWO:
TECH TORMENTS

No one likes it when technology goes on the fritz, but it's common to run into computer issues at work. This chapter includes different ways to use technology to your advantage. These digital tricks will have your coworkers scratching their heads as they try to figure out what's wrong with their devices.

For some, you'll need to know a thing or two about computers. Others are simple and easy to implement without any specialized knowledge. If you're using a Windows computer, follow the instructions in each section. For a Mac, you'll need to do more research on your own.

The key is to know what you're capable of pulling off based on your computer skills. Don't get too ambitious and accidentally damage someone's devices. If you get in over your head, it's okay to admit defeat and ask IT for help setting things back to normal.

You should also stay away from any security-related functions that could compromise your coworker's computer. Your goal is to ruin your coworker's day with a prank, not ruin your career by running afoul of cybersecurity rules.

[11]
INCORRECT
AUTOCORRECT

Autocorrect is famous for misinterpreting words and adding new meanings to even the most boring of conversations. It also gives you the chance to intentionally introduce chaos by sabotaging a coworker's autocorrect settings.

If you're using Microsoft Word, go to *File* and scroll down to *Options*. That should open a new window with *Proofing* on the left-hand side. From there, look for the button that says *AutoCorrect Options*. You should see a table that gives you the option to fill in custom entries. Simply add the words you want to replace and what you want to replace them with.

When your unsuspecting coworker types one of those words, the autocorrect feature will replace it with the term you specified in settings. You can replace just one pair or go all out by swapping multiple words. For example, you might change their name to *Doofus* or turn your company's name into a corny pun.

It's best to make these pranks as obvious as possible. Otherwise, your coworker could inadvertently send a rude or nonsensical email to clients before they notice the autocorrected version. You should also avoid anything too vulgar or rude for a professional setting.

[12]
IN THE
BACKGROUND

Does your coworker have a favorite actor, musician, or other public figure? If so, search for a picture making fun of that person, and set it as the desktop background on your coworker's computer. When they get back to their desk, they'll be shocked to see a joke about their favorite celebrity.

This prank also works well for diehard sports fans. For instance, if your coworker loves the Philadelphia Eagles, change their background to the Dallas Cowboys. Seeing the "enemy" on their screen is sure to evoke a strong reaction.

As you search for memes or photos, steer clear of potentially controversial figures, such as politicians or religious leaders. Taunting coworkers who have different beliefs could cause tensions to spiral out of control.

[13]
UPSIDE DOWN

Turning your coworker's computer desktop upside down is a quick prank that's guaranteed to cause confusion. The only potential hiccup is that their computer needs to be unlocked for you to be able to access their settings.

The process itself is simple. Right click on their desktop and choose *Display settings*. Scroll down to *Display orientation*. On most computers, this will be set to landscape mode. Change it to *Portrait (flipped)* in the drop-down menu. Their desktop should now be completely upside down.

The direction of their mouse will be reversed as well. If they try to move their cursor down, it'll go up toward the taskbar at the top. It's challenging to navigate with a backwards mouse, which will make it even more difficult for your coworker to fix the problem or research a solution.

[14]
THE POLYGLOT
PRANK

Assuming that your coworker isn't an expert polyglot, changing the language on their computer will throw them for a loop. Open the settings menu and select *Time & Language* on the left. Next, click on *Language & Region*. The first block should say *Windows Display Language* and give you the option to set a new default language.

If you don't see any other languages as options, you'll need to add them. Languages like Arabic that have a different written alphabet will have the best visual effect. Before you choose, make sure you know how to change the settings back once the joke is over. After all, unless you speak the language you selected, you won't be able to read the instructions or menu options.

In a worst-case scenario where you can't change the language back, look up an instructional video on a different device and follow the same steps. You won't know what each button says, but the video should have the translations in English as long as they're using the same version of Windows.

[15]
HIDDEN LINKS

Like anyone else, your coworkers have routines and habits at work. They probably don't look too closely at their most-used icons before clicking, since they have their appearance and general location memorized. This tendency makes it easy to swap their browser icon with a shortcut to a funny YouTube video.

The first step is to find the YouTube video you want to use. You could choose something loud or annoying if you just want to give your coworker a shock. There are also countless internet jokes that you could reference, including Rick Astley's "Never Gonna Give You Up" to the world-famous screaming goat video.

After finding the right video, you'll need to create a shortcut through your browser. On Chrome, click the three vertical dots in the top righthand corner to open a new menu. At the bottom, you'll find an option called Cast, Save, and Share. Hover over it, then navigate to the side menu and click Create shortcut.

From there, your computer will save the shortcut to your coworker's desktop. However, the logo will be for YouTube instead of Chrome. Right click on the shortcut and select Properties to open a new window. Click the button that says Change Icon. It will give you the option to choose a new icon instead of the YouTube one that automatically populated.

Unless you already have the Chrome icon saved, the next step is to download the Chrome icon from a site like Iconfinder. Make sure you're downloading the ISO file instead of just a regular PNG or JPEG image. After downloading, return to the settings window and use the Browse button to find the Chrome image file you just saved.

Your desktop shortcut to the YouTube video should now have the Chrome logo. Once you update the name of the shortcut, it should be indistinguishable from the real Chrome icon. You can even pin it to your coworker's taskbar to be extra convincing.

[16]
MASS LAYOFFS

The next time you have a meeting with your boss or a member of upper management, pretend that they gave you advance warning about upcoming layoffs. Put on your best sad face and spin your tale of woe to your coworker. Citing realistic issues, such as rising costs or a botched project, will make your claim even more believable.

If you're convincing, your coworker might panic or ask someone else what they've heard about layoffs. With this in mind, it's better to save this prank for friends and people you know well at work. A coworker who's struggling to make ends meet or provide for a family is unlikely to take the joke well.

You should also recognize when it's time to stop the prank. You don't want the rumor to spread throughout the entire office and cause widespread concern. If you let it go on too long, some of your coworkers could even start looking for other jobs or make other life-changing decisions.

[17]
STATUS UPDATE

Platforms like Microsoft Teams are perfect for pranking. If your office uses a collaboration tool that allows you to set a status, you can sneak over to your coworker's desk and adjust their displayed message. For example, you could change their status from *on break* to *farting up the bathroom.* If your coworker isn't paying close attention to their status, they could inadvertently leave it up for hours or days at a time.

This prank is a safer alternative to sabotaging their email signature or putting up a fake out-of-office message, since it won't affect any clients. Instead, their status will only be visible to other employees.

[18]
HELLO?
PRINTER?

In the age of smart assistants such as Alexa and Siri, it's common to hear people talking to their devices. Besides phones and computers, it's now possible to purchase smart appliances like refrigerators and microwaves. This prank involves tricking your coworkers into believing a traditional piece of office equipment has a new smart assistant.

A communal printer is a good place to start. Add a note that says the printer has been upgraded to include a voice-activated assistant. You can even include a sample script that directs people to phrase their requests in a certain way. Hide around the corner to catch coworkers saying, "Hey, Printer!"

To make the prank extra convincing, ask another coworker to hit print when they hear you talking to the printer. Your other coworkers will see that it works and try it for themselves. They might even approach you to ask for help when they can't get the printer to listen.

[19]
ALPHABET
SOUP

If your coworker uses a traditional keyboard, it's easy to remove the letter caps and switch them around. Simply pop off a few keys and snap them back into place in a random order. While this won't affect coworkers who don't look at their fingers to type, it'll throw off anyone who doesn't have the keyboard memorized.

However, don't try this prank with laptop keys. The keys on laptops aren't easy to remove, and you're likely to break the fragile components underneath. Your coworker won't be happy about having to send their laptop out for repairs, and your boss isn't likely to be pleased about the bill.

[20]
FAKE
DESKTOP

For this prank, you'll need to replace your coworker's desktop with a screenshot. When they go to open a file, it won't work, since their desktop will be a still image instead of functional icons. They'll waste time clicking icons that don't exist and troubleshooting a problem that's bound to be much different than what they expected.

To start, take a screenshot of your coworker's entire desktop. Many computers have a print screen key that will allow you to quickly take a picture. Look for the abbreviation *PrtSc*. If you don't see a print screen button, search for the Snipping Tool. That will allow you to select the area you want to copy.

Save the screenshot somewhere that's easy to find. Next, right click on the desktop and select *Personalize*. From there, select *Background* and *Browse photos*. Retrieve the screenshot you just saved and set it as the background. Your coworker's screen should look roughly the same, since the image is supposed to be an exact copy of their existing desktop.

From there, hide all the desktop icons. Right click and select *View*. Scroll down to the bottom of the next menu and click *Show desktop icons*. All the icons and shortcuts will disappear, leaving only the background image with the fake equivalents.

CHAPTER THREE:

COMMUNICATION CAPERS

Workplaces are full of miscommunications, so it's easy to take advantage by intentionally adding mischief to routine interactions. The pranks in this chapter involve using emails, calls, and other forms of communication to create confusion among your peers.

If you don't have your coworker's contact information, check to see if your company has a directory or a phone list. Another coworker may also be able to put you in touch with your intended target. Just take care to conceal your identity if you're sending anonymous notes or making goofy calls.

Keep in mind that your coworker won't necessarily interpret everything you do as a prank. Avoid sending any questionable messages that could get you in hot water with the law. If you need to make a threat, keep it lighthearted, such as leaving a ransom note for the coffee in the break room.

[21]
YOU'VE GOT
SPAM

People have their own individual preferences and habits, so it's rare to find a universal opinion that broadly applies to just about everyone. Spam emails are an exception to the rule. No matter who you ask, no one enjoys receiving junk mail or unwanted calls.

This prank involves signing your coworker up for spam by filling in lead forms on various websites. Zillow works well for this since realtors are always eager to make a new connection with a prospective client. Look for expensive houses and mansions that are unlikely to attract a lot of attention.

Another option is to sign your coworker up to receive sales calls for products or home upgrades. The next time you pass a salesperson at a kiosk in the mall or a website asks you to sign up for free coupons, put in your coworker's contact details instead. They'll soon be inundated with contact requests and wonder where they came from.

[22]
GOOD
SAMARITAN

Have you ever found a wallet, phone, or other valuable item in public that someone dropped? Searching for the owner is the right thing to do, and many people will go out of their way to track them down. You can capitalize on this behavior by making fake sets of lost keys and putting your coworker's number on the keychain.

Custom key chains are available through platforms such as Etsy and Zazzle. Add your coworker's phone number to the design. If there's space, you could also add their first name. It's best to leave off their last name to protect their privacy.

Once you have the key chains, it's fairly cheap to buy scrap keys on websites like eBay. These look more realistic, since they're worn and heavy. Pop a few on each key chain and start dropping them around town wherever you go. You can also hide them around your workplace for other coworkers to find and bring back to their "owner."

[23]
PLAY
ON PUNS

This next prank is perfect for jobs that require following up on leads or calls from customers. Fill out a lead form or leave a sticky note with a fake name and a phone number to a real place. Make the name a pun that relates to the place they're calling. For example, leave your coworker a note to call Mr. Lyon and include the number for the zoo.

You could also include references to fake people with funny names in meeting minutes or other notes. Your coworkers will embarrass themselves by asking about the status of Chris P. Bacon's account.

[24]
WHAT'S IN
A NAME?

If you have a name that can be spelled in a variety of ways, try throwing off your coworkers by signing your emails with different spellings each time. The name *Katherine* could be *Katie*, *Kathy*, *Kait*, *Kat*, or any other number of other options. This joke works particularly well with new employees, since they won't know everyone's name already.

For names that only have a couple of spellings, add nicknames to the rotation to make a longer list. Choose absurd monikers or references to inside jokes to get your coworkers laughing. Just remember to use your formal name for anything that might get forwarded to clients or your boss.

[25]
GRAMMAR
POLICE

It's common to make spelling and grammatical errors in emails or chat, especially if you're informally discussing a project with coworkers. You can prank your coworkers by becoming the "grammar police" and correcting all their minor mistakes. If anyone asks, claim that you've developed an obsession with grammar and you want to share your newfound passion with your friends.

To make the situation even funnier, let some of your coworkers in on the joke. This way, it'll seem like the entire group is suddenly obsessed with spelling and grammar. The people who don't know what's going on might even change their mannerisms to become more proper.

[26]
DEFINE THAT

Every job has its own lingo, including abbreviations, acronyms, and standardized phrases. Choose a term your coworker uses often, and pretend you suddenly don't understand it. Ask them for an explanation. A few minutes later, pick a different word and pretend you don't know the definition for that one either.

This prank fits just about any work environment. Whether you're in a traditional office setting or working on a construction site, it shouldn't be hard to pick out jargon in routine conversations. While you can also adapt this trick to email, it's funnier when you can see the person's facial expressions when you ask them to define basic terms.

[27]
EASY READER

The next time a coworker sends you a report or a long email, pretend you don't understand what it's trying to say. Ask them to rewrite it in a simpler format, and mention that you're not great at understanding complicated messages. It'll make them second-guess whether they went overboard or used complicated terminology.

For example, mention that you have trouble understanding terms with more than three syllables. You'll know your prank worked if their emails suddenly have shorter words that meet your new restriction.

[28]
WACKY WORDS

If your workplace isn't big on email, you can still prank your coworkers by mispronouncing ordinary words in day-to-day interactions. For example, turning *parking lot* into *parking loot* will definitely earn you a few odd looks. Continue to escalate the joke to see how long it takes your coworkers to correct you or ask about your strange pronunciations.

For an ongoing prank, convince other coworkers to join in with your strange pronunciations. The remaining people in the room might even change their speech patterns or look up the pronunciation to see if they've been saying common words wrong their entire lives.

[29]
CRY FOR HELP

Some pranks require more setup than others, and this one will require a little outside support. Check in with your IT department to see if they can make you a second email account with your company's official domain. Choose a vague username with initials or other details that can't be traced back to you.

After your new account is live, add a fake name and job title to your email signature. Use that account to message a coworker and introduce yourself as a new hire. This works best if you pretend to be a remote employee who isn't in the office on a regular basis.

Once you've established contact, start making bizarre requests or asking strange questions. At first, your coworker will probably do their best to be helpful, but eventually, their goodwill is bound to run out. You can further stoke the flames by complaining about your fake persona and telling your coworker that you're receiving weird emails, too.

This prank is most effective with small teams or workplaces where you have a good relationship with your supervisor.

This way, if your coworker complains to management about the new hire, you can confess to the joke without getting yourself in trouble.

[30]
COOL TUNES

Instead of making a traditional prank call, this joke involves playing an annoying song into the receiver every time your coworker picks up. It's even more effective if your coworker needs to answer any incoming calls as part of their job description.

You can research songs that are likely to get stuck in someone's head, or go on YouTube to find a compilation of irritating noises. The next step is to find a spare phone in an empty office or a communal phone that anyone can use. Otherwise, your coworker will be able to see where the call is coming from and trace it back to you.

If you decide to confess to your antics, walk into your coworker's area, playing the same song or noise you used on the phone. They'll instantly recognize it and demand to know why you're playing that song.

CHAPTER FOUR:

SURPRISE SHENANIGANS

Nothing ruins a day like an unexpected "gift." The pranks in this chapter include unpleasant surprises and gags that will keep your coworkers on their toes. Unlike technology-focused pranks, many of these jokes can be carried out away from computers and phones. Feel free to use your imagination to tailor them to your work environment.

Just bear in mind that unpleasant surprises can lead to unpredictable results. There's no way to know how your coworkers will react in the moment. Steer clear of any shenanigans that could be misconstrued as harassment or threatening behavior. For example, your coworkers might get upset if you start using their personal contact information for pranks.

[31]
DELIVERY
NOTES

The next time you want to torment your coworker, consider ordering them delivery with a mean message attached. Picture their face when they accept the order, only to see an unexpected insult like *you suck* or *I hate you* written on the front. Flowers will have the biggest emotional impact if you can afford to splurge, but you can also order food or coffee.

This prank won't fit every situation, since it's a bit of a double-edged sword. After all, you're cheering someone up and putting them down at the same time. Once they get over the shock of seeing an insult on the bag or card, they still walk away with free lunch and a funny story to share with the office.

It's also easy to adapt a delivery prank to different situations. If a coworker is leaving for a new job, pretend you always wanted them to quit anyway. For birthdays, make fun of them for getting old. Most delivery services will allow any kind of custom message, so you can add snarky comments without fear that the company will object.

[32]
FORBIDDEN
ENTRY

Blocking the entrance to your coworker's cubicle is a low-tech, simple prank that's easy to put together in just a few minutes. One option is to build a fake wall out of empty boxes. You could also pile bags of shredded paper in the entryway.

Covering doorways with plastic wrap is another well-known joke online, but people are likely to get hurt if they walk face first into an invisible barrier without warning. Adding sticky notes or pieces of paper will make it more obvious while still creating an inconvenience for your coworker. Plus, using paper gives you the chance to include a frowny face or a mean message on the outside.

If you have rope or string at your disposal, weaving a barrier across the entrance will slow your coworker down as they try to return to their desk. You can do this as part of the cubicle maze prank mentioned previously, or as a standalone joke.

[33]
SPARKLE AND SHINE

When you truly want to make your coworker miserable, give them a letter filled with glitter. Not only will they have to read your rude message, but they'll also be covered in sparkles that seem impossible to remove. This prank even has a special name after gaining popularity as a prank and form of political protest: glitter bombing.

Believe it not, there are even businesses that will ship different types of glitter bombs to your enemies. Ship Your Enemies Glitter offers glitter-filled cards and spring-loaded glitter bombs. Using a formal service is probably going overboard for a workplace joke, but it's an option if you don't want to organize it yourself.

To soften the blow, consider leaving a lint roller or a roll of packing tape to help your coworker remove the glitter from their clothes. Plus, if your workplace has carpet, they can use the sticky tape to pick up any glitter that falls on the floor, instead of leaving a mess for the custodial staff or closing shift.

[34]
BOOBY TRAPS

If your coworker has a separate office with a door that closes, you can set up booby traps on the other side to catch them by surprise. A simple option is to hang a bucket over the door that will spill when they open it. Fill the bucket with confetti or shredded paper. There are plenty of instructional videos on YouTube if you're not sure how to rig up the trap.

The hard part is making sure the right person triggers the trap. The last thing you want is for your boss to go into someone's office and accidentally get covered in glitter. It's a good idea to watch the door carefully and intercept anyone who's inadvertently interfering with your shenanigans.

Use care if you opt for messier alternatives, such as syrup, water, or slime. Not only do you risk ruining your coworker's clothes, but they'll also need to go home and change unless they have a spare outfit at the office. With a big enough mess, you'll also be on the hook for cleaning the carpet or scrubbing the tile.

[35]
FAKE RICHES

Pranking your friends with fake money is a classic trick, but people will also be naturally suspicious of seeing random bills out in the open. Make sure your fake bills look convincing from a distance. Write a sarcastic note on the back of each, making fun of the person for being gullible. Then drop them in the parking lot or around your workplace.

If you want to take your joke to the next level, there are fake scratch-off lottery tickets that always reveal a big win. These tickets are designed to look as realistic as possible. Mix them in with a few real ones from the store and give them to your coworker for a special occasion. Just keep in mind that not everyone will react well to this type of joke, especially if they're going through tough times with money.

[36]
SWEET TOOTH

Bringing in sweets and snacks to share with the office is a common gesture that brightens up the day. Since your goal is to torment your coworkers instead, try bringing in an empty box to make it seem like everyone just missed out on the last treat. Doughnut boxes work well since they're distinct, but you can also use boxes from snack packs or even pizza.

If you're truly diabolical, leave out a candy dish with an unusual mix of items. For instance, you could mix together Skittles and M&Ms to shock anyone who grabs a handful in passing. Putting cough drops in a dish of hard candy works, too, but it's only funny if someone realizes it's a cough drop after the fact.

This kind of prank also works well if your coworker is out of the office for a day, preferably for a boring activity like mandatory training. Fill the office with pizza boxes, ice cream cartons, and other goodies. When they come back the next day, tell them all about how they missed an unannounced party for employee appreciation.

[37]
WHO FARTED?

Leaving a whoopee cushion on your coworker's chair is such an old-fashioned joke that they might not see it coming. The key is to choose a place your coworker will sit down automatically, without paying much attention to what's on the seat. Their desk chair or a conference chair should be good options, since sitting down in those locations is likely to be second nature.

If you don't think you'll be able to catch your target unaware, hide the whoopee cushion under a seat cover. Many office chairs have a removable cover that unzips on the side. There should be just enough space, since whoopee cushions aren't particularly large.

Obviously, your coworker will know mischief is afoot as soon as they find your surprise addition to their chair. If other coworkers think it's funny, hiding the whoopee cushion could even become a recurring joke whenever there's a meeting in your department.

[38]
OFFICE WARS

You'll need to recruit some coconspirators to pull off this prank. The first step is to buy rubber toys that can be shot from your finger like a slingshot. These "flinger" toys are perfect for the workplace, since they don't resemble an actual slingshot and don't fire any kind of separate projectile. Look for the ones that are shaped like rubber chickens for an extra laugh.

Next, distribute them around the office and tell your coworkers to shoot them at a particular person as they pass. Your coworker will constantly be looking over their shoulder to see if anyone is taking aim. If they manage to steal a few finger slingshots for themselves, it could turn into a full-on war.

[39]
FACE YOUR FEARS

Does your coworker have a well-known phobia, such as being afraid of spiders? If so, buy a toy replica and hide it somewhere like a desk drawer. You could also sneak them into your coworker's bag or drop one into their jacket pocket when they're not around.

There are also remote-controlled spiders and mice, if you don't mind spending a few bucks to make your prank even more jarring. Most people will panic if they see a dark shape running across the floor. Since these toys often look realistic enough from a distance, you shouldn't have to worry about anyone identifying them as fakes until they're only a couple of feet away.

Their reaction will depend on the severity of their phobia. When you're looking for potential hiding places, avoid putting prank items in dangerous places. For example, hiding a fake mouse inside a forklift could cause a serious accident.

[40]
MYSTERIOUS
MESSAGES

Have you seen the movie *I Know What You Did Last Summer*? This prank involves leaving ominous messages for your coworker to see if you can spook them into revealing their secrets. Leave them a note—or a voicemail, if you're feeling ambitious—that claims to know about their past misdeeds.

With vague wording, like *I know what you did*, your message could apply to just about anything. If they bring it up to you, pick their brain to see if they're willing to speculate about the cause. You could learn some shocking new information, or at least good workplace gossip, in the process.

Remember to disguise your handwriting or voice to keep them from guessing who left the message. You can even go one step beyond by cutting out letters from magazines and leaving a ransom-style note.

[41]
IN MOTION

For this prank, you'll need to buy a set of motion-activated devices that play funny noises or offer the chance to add your own. Stick them around the office in doorways and walkways to scare your coworkers. Motion-activated doorbells can also work in a pinch.

Periodically moving the devices to new locations will keep the joke fresh. On the other hand, your prank could become an ongoing source of entertainment if everyone knows to expect a funny noise at a specific time. For example, leaving a sensor that makes a fart noise in the doorway of the bathroom will add some humor to routine bathroom breaks.

CHAPTER FIVE:

OFFICE OBSTACLES

Instead of always bringing in outside items to mess with your coworkers, you can use the existing furniture and supplies to stage your pranks. Not only will that be more convenient for you, but it'll also keep you from alerting your coworkers to your evil plans. After all, if they know you're the office joker and you're coming into work with a bag of materials, they're bound to be suspicious.

The jokes in this chapter involve physical obstacles. They can be carried out with only a few items from home or a trip to the supply closet. You'll need to use your creativity to figure out the best way to position furniture or borrow equipment from around the office.

Just be careful about what you block off. Don't interfere with emergency exits, bathrooms, or safety equipment. Similarly, avoid setting up physical pranks in such a way that someone could get seriously injured. If you cause a workplace injury or damage property, it could cost you your job, even if you had good intentions.

[42]
CUBICLE
MAZE

This prank takes some time to set up, so you may want to wait until your coworker has gone home for the day. Use yarn, twine, or string to create a maze in their cubicle. Imagine that a laser is bouncing off each wall.

Desk drawers, filing cabinet handles, and armrests are all great places to secure the string. Add push pins or tape if you want to make it more complex. When your coworker returns in the morning, they won't even be able to get back into their cubicle!

If you want to prank more than one person, run the string through both of their cubicles. That will make it even more challenging to unravel. You can also hide their scissors to make them hunt for another way to cut the string.

[43]
BALLOON
ROOM

Balloons are easy to sneak in when they aren't inflated. Bring a manual air pump to fill them up once you're out of sight. Since only helium balloons rise, you can fill a coworker's cubicle without balloons floating away. If you have a lot of time on your hands, it may even be possible to fill an entire conference room without anyone noticing.

If the doors in your office have windows, tape balloons over the glass from the inside. That will make people think all the rooms have been filled. You can also go into some of the empty rooms and pretend they're stuffed to the ceiling.

[44]
CRIME SCENE

Block off your coworker's area and make it look like a crime scene. Stretch crime scene tape across the doorway and put props on the floor. Online kits typically include numbered plastic signs, a chalk outline of a body, and fake blood. While none of it will look realistic, it'll still be an amusing way to torment your coworker by disrupting their normal routine.

If it's close to Halloween, a crime scene joke may even seem festive. You can add decorations from the Halloween store and go all-out with accessories. Another option is to wait until your coworker reaches a major achievement, such as "killing" the competition with a new project. Drawing and labeling a chalk outline with the other company's name will get a good laugh and show that you appreciate their hard work.

[45]
FURNITURE
SWAP

Rearranging the furniture in your office building is enough to ruin someone's day on its own, but you can also create physical obstacles out of the things you move. For instance, if you remove all the chairs from the conference room, go one step further and push them into the break room to block the microwave.

The possibilities are endless if you use your imagination. Before long, you'll be blocking the vending machine with filing cabinets and crowding your coworkers' cubicles with all the fake plants. In addition to getting in everyone's way, your coworkers will also need to carry the items back to their original locations.

[46]
OUT OF ORDER

Ready to cause real mayhem? Start by unplugging random pieces of equipment around the office. Put up signs that say they're due for maintenance or out of order, but don't specify when they're expected to be fixed. Choose high-traffic targets, such as the coffeemaker, printer, or vacuum cleaner.

Don't go too overboard, or people will quickly see through the ruse. Enjoy listening to your coworkers' gripes as they attempt to work around the "broken" appliances. They may even call IT to troubleshoot the problem, only to discover that nothing is plugged in.

However, it's best to avoid tampering with any safety or emergency equipment, even if you don't anticipate needing it in the near future. Items like the defibrillator should always be off-limits. You should also skip over the refrigerator, since you don't want to inadvertently give anyone food poisoning.

[47]
SHRINKING
THE OFFICE

Take a good look at your coworker's cubicle or office. Note the items they have inside, including the furniture and any personal effects, such as picture frames. Next, go online or head to your local craft store to search for miniature versions of your coworker's furniture. Toy stores may also sell miniature housewares and accessories for dolls.

Buy the items that match the ones in your coworker's area. Remove the real furniture and replace it with the models. Imagine how silly it will look to put a tiny chair in front of their full-size desk or a doll's computer in place of their actual laptop. Plus, for extra inconvenience, your coworkers will have to figure out where you hid their real furniture before they can start their day.

[48]
LABEL IT

You'll need a lot of labeling tape for this next prank. Instead of rearranging your coworker's stuff, use a label maker to name every object in their cubicle. Label their monitor, clipboard, and phone.

Get down to the details to be as aggravating as possible. Open their drawers and label each individual paper clip and pen. For peak irritation, put redundant labels over things like calculator buttons that are already clearly marked.

Once you're done in their cubicle, you could go label their lunch bag in the refrigerator or stick a label on their car window. If you prank multiple people and want to continue the joke, label the soap dispenser in the bathroom and the flusher on the toilet.

[49]
PARKING FINES

If your company has a parking lot, you can wreak havoc by giving out fake parking tickets. Joke shops sell generic versions that come in high-visibility colors with envelopes. Stick them under your coworker's windshield wipers and watch from a nearby window as they head out to their car at the end of the day.

For custom parking tickets, check Etsy for an editable parking ticket template. That will make your tickets look more credible, since they'll have a location and company name at the top. You could even pretend your parking lot is now covered by a security firm, and list your own phone number as the payment department for extra laughs.

[50]
WET FLOOR

It's basic safety to put up a "wet floor" sign after mopping or a spill. Therefore, most workplaces keep a few on hand, especially if your building has hard flooring. Find one of these signs and start leaving them in nonsensical places, like carpeted break areas or a patch of grass. Your coworkers will be baffled and wonder who's moving the signs around.

You can also purchase fake spills that look like blood or oil. While it's normal to see water or cleaner on the floor, it'll shock your coworkers to realize that someone left a dangerous substance out in the open instead of cleaning it up.

CHAPTER SIX:

FOOD FOLLIES

Ready to cause culinary chaos? This chapter includes food-related pranks that target your coworkers' meals and snacks. Since most workplaces have a break area with a communal refrigerator, you'll have your choice of people to prank. Plus, with everyone cycling in and out of the break room at different times, it'll be harder to catch you in the act.

Once you start sabotaging your coworkers' food, look closely before you dig into your own lunch. Your peers might catch on to your misdeeds and retaliate when you least expect it. Just keep in mind that not everyone will appreciate you tampering with their food. If you know that someone has a food allergy or keeps medicine in their lunchbox, turn your focus somewhere else.

Your pranks shouldn't put anyone in actual danger. It's also important to note that these jokes aren't intended for restaurants where your antics could impact the general public. Even if you're working away from customers, commercial kitchens are still regulated differently. The last thing you need is the health inspector to show up because someone misinterpreted a prank.

[51]
HELP
YOURSELF

The next time you notice a tasty meal in the fridge, eat it and leave your coworker a note thanking them for their thoughtfulness. You can even write them a formal card that explains how much you enjoyed it. When they confront you, pretend that you thought they were bringing in food for the entire office.

This prank is best reserved for close friends who won't get angry or file a complaint. You should also be prepared to reimburse your coworker or take them out for lunch. They might think your joke is funny but still need something to eat for the day.

[52]
SHAKEN UP

Many employees rely on caffeine to make it through the day. If your coworker keeps soda or energy drinks in the fridge, shake them up and put them back as ticking time bombs.

When they go to open their caffeine fix, they'll find themselves soaking wet instead.

Timing is important to make sure this prank goes off without a hitch. You may need to observe your coworker's habits for a few days to get a sense of their routine. For example, if you realize they always grab an energy drink after they eat lunch, you'll know exactly when to sneak into the kitchen and shake up their day.

This prank is great for catered lunches, where carbonated beverages are on a communal table. Head to the event early and shake a few of the sodas before anyone else arrives. A few unlucky people will get soaked, and you can always claim that someone must have dropped the cans.

[53]
SUGAR SWAP

If your office kitchen has a salt shaker, pour out the salt and replace it with sugar. Your coworkers will inadvertently ruin their own lunches, and you'll have plausible deniability that you knew anything was wrong. The opposite also works if you'd rather replace the sugar in a communal dish with salt.

That'll ruin your coworker's cup of coffee and send them on the hunt for the actual sugar.

It's a little more complicated if your office only has individually wrapped sugar or salt packets. Depending on your dedication to the prank, you may be able to replace the contents and glue the edges back together. Your coworkers will be less likely to suspect individual packets if they believe they're still sealed from the factory.

[54]
EXTRA
PROTEIN

While leaving a fake bug in your coworker's lunch bag might seem too juvenile, the simplest pranks are sometimes the most effective. Your coworker won't be expecting someone to play such a goofy joke, so they'll automatically think it's a real bug.

Search around for realistic fake bugs that would also reasonably be living in the kitchen. Cockroaches, for instance, are attracted to food and will almost certainly gross someone out. A cricket, on the other hand, probably isn't going to evoke the same reaction.

You could also put a fake worm into your coworker's salad or sandwich. While that would be significantly more upsetting, it also means you'll need to touch their food directly. Even if you wear gloves, not everyone will want to eat something after you've touched it, regardless of whether the bug is real.

[55]
PLAY KITCHEN

Toy stores often sell play food to go with children's kitchen sets. Buy a bag and keep common items, such as fruit and sandwiches, on hand. When your coworker brings in a matching item, swap it out with the plastic toy version. At a glance, they may not even realize their food is missing until they get deeper into their lunchbox.

Meanwhile, leave their real sandwich inside a toy picnic basket or hide it under a pile of other fake foods. They'll need to go back to the kitchen to figure out what happened to their actual lunch. If they leave their empty lunchbox in the break area, replace the entire bag with a toy lunchbox for dolls.

[56]
CANDIED
"APPLES"

Candied apples are colorful, versatile, and delicious. They can be made with plain caramel or more complex toppings, such as candy pieces. Most people don't scrutinize candied apples too closely, since they're a known quantity. They're a bit heavy and smell sweet on the outside. They may also have an irregular shape, since apples are all different shapes and sizes.

You can take advantage of their assumptions by swapping the apple with another round fruit or vegetable. Make sure it has a similar consistency and isn't too squishy to be convincing. Using an onion is particularly awful because of its acrid flavor.

Of course, this prank will require some do-it-yourself skills to pull off. You'll need to buy supplies to actually make the "apples" at home. Check the baking aisle or your local craft store for treat sticks and meltable candy coatings. You may also want to create some real candied apples to make your coworkers more trusting before getting to a prank "apple" in the middle of the batch.

Once your fake apples are ready, wrap them in plastic or store them in the refrigerator at work. That will keep them from melting or starting to smell. You can also leave a sign telling your coworkers to help themselves if you want to carry out the prank without getting caught.

[57]
SCAVENGER
HUNT

For this prank, steal your coworker's snack or lunch, and create an elaborate treasure hunt for them to retrieve it. Leave clues throughout the building to keep them on their toes. You can include riddles, inside jokes, or quiz questions they need to answer to find the location of the next clue.

If you want to hide their snacks in a new area, such as a nearby park, you could make a treasure map instead of using clues. They'll need to navigate to the right area and find landmarks to locate their food. Encode some of the clues as riddles to increase the difficulty.

Just make sure not to hide any food that's perishable. A granola bar can sit out all day, while a container with chicken won't last more than an hour or two without being refrigerated. The length of the hunt is entirely up to you, but you don't want to make the prank so prolonged that your coworker doesn't have time to eat. This is especially true if your company tracks the length of lunch breaks.

[58]
WARNING
SIGNS

Write a quick note that says *do not eat* and stick it to your coworker's lunchbox. Include a silly reason that will make them hesitate before eating. You could claim that someone dropped it on the floor or coughed all over their sandwich. Watch them from a distance to see if they believe the note.

If you keep up the joke for too long, they'll stop believing your warnings. Keep things fresh by carrying through on some of your threats, like filling their lunchbox with gummy worms or doodling on the outside of their banana. This way, they won't know whether your note is actually a warning or just a joke.

Be respectful if your coworker asks you to stop using their lunch in pranks. They may have a food sensitivity or another serious reason for wanting you to leave their food alone. It could be as simple as needing a legitimate break to mentally reset before going back to work after lunch.

[59]
WATERCOOLER

If your workplace has a watercooler, sneak in a bottle of vinegar, fill up one of the empty water jugs, and place it back on the dispenser. This prank also works for individual water bottles. When your coworker goes to get a drink, they'll soon be spitting and sputtering. Vinegar has such a strong flavor that they'll be tasting it all day.

Bear in mind that vinegar also has a strong smell. You may want to dilute it with water to minimize the smell and keep it from alerting your coworkers to the switch. Additionally, diluting the vinegar will minimize the risk of it staining the carpet or your coworkers' clothes.

[60]
COFFEE SWAP

For workplaces with a traditional coffee pot instead of a Keurig-style coffeemaker, it's easy to replace the caffeinated grounds with decaf. Simply switch the contents of the containers and put them back on the shelf. If your office only has caffeinated coffee, buy some decaf and smuggle it into work.

You'll get a giggle from watching everyone yawn and lose focus throughout the day. You can even hint that something is amiss by making comments like, "Everyone looks so worn out lately!" Drawing attention to the issue could inspire your coworkers to seek out more coffee, which further compounds the joke.

This prank definitely won't make you any friends. People are passionate about their coffee, so interfering with their caffeine fix is sure to be seen as the ultimate betrayal. Don't be surprised if your coworkers refuse to drink anything you offer them again. At least you'll be off the hook for making coffee for the rest of your career.

CHAPTER SEVEN:

MEETING MISCHIEF

Whether you work in a huge commercial building or log in from your couch, no one enjoys going to meetings. The long-standing joke that a meeting could have been an email is often true. Between coworkers who ramble and repetitive issues that never get resolved, it's no wonder that you want to add some levity to the situation.

The pranks in this chapter are meant to disrupt everyday meetings and introduce some chaos to an otherwise boring activity. Most of them can be adapted to in-person or work-from-home environments with a little creativity. It may just be more difficult to avoid detection if you leave behind a digital signature.

Additionally, it's important to confirm exactly who will be at a meeting before you set up a joke. You don't want to fill the conference room with balloons, only to realize an external client is about to arrive. It's also dangerous to meddle with formal meetings, especially if it's your annual performance review.

[61]
ABSURD
INVITATIONS

Instead of meeting up with your friends at the watercooler, send an invite for a real meeting with a ridiculous purpose. Topics could include recent sporting events, cat pictures, or what to buy for the snack cabinet. Send the invitation to your coworkers and see who joins.

The benefit of this prank is that it works equally well for in-person and remote teams. As more companies shift to hybrid schedules, you won't have to forego pranking your work-from-home peers. You'll just need to fill in a different description that won't give away the true purpose of the meeting.

Your fake event will be even more amusing if you conduct it like an actual meeting. Imagine asking your coworker to take meeting minutes for an in-depth discussion on everyone's favorite memes. Assign action items to add authenticity and make your next fake meeting more "productive."

[62]
PRESENTATION MODIFICATION

Instead of using your coworker's professional presentation, change their slides to include weird colors and joke images. Leave the title slide the same, so that it looks normal when it's loaded up on the screen. Sneak into the conference room in advance of their presentation and launch your joke version. They'll be stunned when they progress to the next slide and realize it isn't what they originally created.

Depending on the setting and the people in attendance, your prank presentation could be a big hit. Some coworkers might think it's more entertaining to include funny pictures or the latest slang. After all, it's common for modern marketing teams to use informal language and humor in advertising. You might start a new trend without intending to!

[63]
DRESS CODE

You'll need some collaboration to pull off this prank. Talk to your coworkers and arrange for everyone to wear the same outfit or similar colors to a meeting. It's especially effective if you're going to a large gathering, such as an all-hands meeting or a company-wide outing. Anyone who doesn't get the message will stick out like a sore thumb.

If your boss or another prominent member of your organization usually wears a particular style, you can all agree to emulate their look. For example, if your manager is known for wearing floral dresses and long earrings, convince your coworkers to wear something similar on the same day. Buying clothes from the thrift store should keep the costs to a minimum.

[64]
MEAN
MINUTES

During your next meeting, volunteer to be the person who takes meeting minutes. In addition to recording what's going on, include your own snarky jokes. Your coworkers will laugh when they read your sarcastic feedback. If you don't want to put them in the main body of the minutes, use comment boxes to keep your jokes separate. That way, people can resolve the comments if they need an official copy.

Just be cautious about how much you poke fun at potentially sensitive issues. While it's okay to joke about situations or projects that have gone awry, your coworkers probably won't take kindly to comments about their insights or personalities. People may stop inviting you to meetings altogether if you can't take them seriously when it matters.

[65]
COMPANY
AWARDS

Recognition is an important part of corporate life, so your coworkers may not recognize when an award is completely fake. You can simply invent your own award, give it a realistic name, and present a certificate to the recipient at a special meeting. Everyone will think it's a valid award that was approved by someone else.

This prank could go far with a little creativity. After the award ceremony, take a picture of the recipient and have a print made. Frame it and hang it on the wall with a plaque and the name of the award. If you get away with it, wait a year and award it to someone new. Before long, you'll have multiple recipients featured in a prominent place of honor for an award that doesn't exist.

Over time, leaders will quit or retire, so newcomers won't know that the award isn't real. When you're approaching another annual award period, invite new leaders to a meeting to vote on the next recipient. Add bizarre criteria and performance metrics to see how long you can keep the ruse going.

[66]
SOUND
EFFECTS

Download a set of sound effects on your phone to play during meetings and other company events. Sounds like applause will likely get some laughter, while fart noises are a little riskier in the workplace. If you don't want anyone to know you're responsible, get a Bluetooth speaker and hide it somewhere in the room. You can play sound effects from your device without your coworkers being able to tell.

Another option is to download sound effects that are related to your profession. Choose a word as a trigger and play a sound anytime someone says it. For example, you could play a sad clown noise whenever your coworkers say the word *regulations*.

[67]
SCHEDULE
CHAOS

Use a fake email account to duplicate real meetings at different times or days of the week. Your coworkers will come to the meeting, only to realize that it isn't the official one. Inevitably, someone important will be unable to make it, or half the invitees will show up to a different time. It'll create chaos over which invitations are real and when meetings are supposed to happen.

For especially gullible coworkers, include meeting invites for evening hours and weekends. Make the purpose something that's obviously fake to see who you can fool. Of course, you'll also need to log in and waste some of your own personal time, but it'll be worth it if you can pull off the prank.

[68]
PERSONAL
AGENDA

The next time you're invited to a meeting, replace the official agenda with a joke one. You can alter the original agenda to include a few fake elements or pretend that someone accidentally uploaded the wrong document. If you want to make fun of a particular coworker, attach a to-do list of embarrassing tasks, such as calling a cleaning company to ask about toilet stains.

You could even email your department to tell them not to open the attachment, since someone sent you the wrong document by mistake. That almost guarantees that others will open your fake to-do list to see what it's all about. They'll immediately assume that your coworker mislabeled a personal document full of humiliating details.

[69]
PET DAY

Start a rumor that pets are allowed in the office on a particular day that has a meeting scheduled. Most pet owners will jump at the chance to spend the day with their furry friends. You can even design "Bring Your Pet to Work Day" fliers to hang on the wall or distribute via email. Make the fliers as convincing as possible, and emphasize that all animals are welcome.

Your managers will be baffled when people show up to the meeting with their dogs, cats, or other pets. If they complain or say that the event isn't real, retrieve one of the fliers and show it to them. With a little luck, you'll start a new tradition for pet owners at your workplace.

If you want to include people who aren't pet owners, bring a few rocks to work and label them as pet rocks. Leave them around the office for others to pick up if they want to participate. You could also distribute "invisible dog" harnesses that stay upright on a leash and give the appearance that they're on a real dog. Your coworkers will look ridiculous taking their invisible pets for a walk.

[70]
BIRTHDAY
SURPRISES

Instead of rigging up an unpleasant surprise like a bucket of slime over the door, stage a fake birthday surprise for your coworker during an upcoming meeting. Decorate the room with banners and distribute party hats ahead of time. You can even hide if there's enough space in the conference room or nearby areas to conceal the other people in the meeting.

When you all leap out to wish your coworker happy birthday, they'll certainly be surprised. After all, it won't really be their birthday. They may play along to avoid ruining the moment or put a stop to the festivities if they think it's a case of mistaken identity. Either way, it'll cause enough of a disruption to your everyday routine to laugh about later.

This prank requires more coordination than most, since you'll need to buy party decorations and other props ahead of time. If you want to go all out, consider buying a birthday cake with the person's name. You'll also need to inform your other coworkers about the surprise and get everyone into position before your target arrives for what they think is an ordinary meeting.

CHAPTER EIGHT:

CAR CAPERS

For coworkers who drive, cars are a prime target. It's easy to sneak out to the parking area when everyone else is busy, especially if your workplace has a large lot or a separate garage for employees. If your coworkers park on the street, make sure you have the right vehicle and you aren't accidentally targeting an innocent bystander with a similar make and model.

The tricks in this chapter explain how to prank people's vehicles with minimal risk of damage. Use your best judgment when choosing a target and materials. Avoid vehicles that are specialized or particularly valuable. Not only will they be more expensive to repair if something goes wrong, but the owners are also more likely to be protective of their cars.

In these situations, it may be worthwhile to wear a camera and record your pranks as you're carrying them out. That way, no one can accuse you of damaging their vehicle, since you'll have a clear record of the original condition of the car. It'll also be funny to replay the videos later if your coworkers want to know how you pulled off a particular prank.

Be careful about pranking company vehicles. There's a big difference between leaving a goofy note on a coworker's window and writing on a company vehicle that needs to have a professional look. You should also stay away from heavy equipment, since pranks could cause a serious injury or malfunction.

Similarly, don't mess with someone's rental car unless you're willing to cover the bill for a cleaning fee or incidental damage. While you won't always be able to identify a rental car on sight, they often have stickers on the window that remind customers not to smoke. When in doubt, pick another vehicle as your target.

[71]
HONK AND
WAVE

From stick-figure families to funny slogans, it's common to see cars with bumper stickers, magnets, and decals on the back. For this prank, you'll add your own decorations to your coworker's vehicle and encourage other drivers to join in on the joke. For example, you could write *Honk and wave!* on your coworker's back windshield in neon window marker. Another option is to write a mean message about your local sports team to see if you can rile up fans on the road.

While you're choosing your next victim, look for someone who's backed into their parking space. That will make it easier to add a message to their bumper or rear windshield without them noticing. A magnet is the fastest, since you can quickly slap it on someone's car, but a window marker gives you the opportunity to draw your own designs.

Decals and stickers are a bit riskier. Even if they say they're removable, adhesive could damage the paint on your coworker's car. Fixing paint can cost hundreds or even thousands of dollars, so it's probably not worth the gamble.

[72]
WHAT'S
THAT SMELL?

While it sounds absurd, there is such a thing as fart spray. Besides smelling as awful as its name suggests, it's also hard to clean up once you've touched the liquid. Putting fart spray on your coworker's door handle guarantees that they'll be stuck with the stink all the way home. The stench will be even worse if they touch something absorbent, like their seat cushion, before realizing they've been pranked.

To make the prank worse, you can use the rest of the fart spray indoors around the same coworker. Put fart spray on the handles of their filing cabinets or spritz some as soon as they walk by. Before long, your peers will start to complain about the smell and blame your coworker for stinking up the office.

[73]
HIDDEN HORN

Nothing will make your coworker jump like a horn blasting as soon as they start backing out of their parking spot. The trick is to hide a horn underneath their tire that makes a noise as soon as they reverse. Look for an old-fashioned horn with a rubber bulb on the end. Set it just behind their passenger rear tire. You may also be able to use an air horn if you can wedge it in place at just the right angle.

If finding a specific type of horn is too difficult, substitute it with an inflated balloon. When your coworker hears the balloon pop, they'll think it's a flat tire and get out to investigate. It won't be as jarring as a horn, but it'll still stall your coworker on their way home. They'll also experience the frustration of thinking they have a flat tire, only to realize that it's a corny joke at their expense.

[74]
DRIVING SCHOOL

Most people give a wide berth to student drivers and show them extra patience. Because of this, it's common for driving schools to put magnets or signs on their cars in prominent places. However, you can also order your own decals and use them to make your coworkers seem like a novice on the road.

This prank will get a ton of laughs if you wait until someone gets into a fender bender. If they're still driving the same vehicle to work, put the sign next to the dent on their car. Hiding the sign on the passenger side will also reduce the chances that your coworker will see it before they drive away.

[75]
FAKE
DAMAGE

You don't have to cause real damage to your coworker's vehicle to ruin their day. Joke shops sell removable fake scratches that you can easily affix to their car to make it seem like it's down to the bare metal. There are also prank window clings with a spidering pattern that resembles broken glass. Some even include half a tennis ball that will look like it's lodged in your coworker's windshield.

[76]
MYSTERY
MISHAP

Leave an anonymous note on your coworker's car apologizing for "the damage." Don't specify what happened or indicate where the damage could be. Claim that you don't have insurance, and that's why you're not including contact information.

Your coworker will waste time looking for dents and scratches that don't exist. If they do happen to find coincidental damage, it'll ruin their entire day. They'll be furious that someone got away with hitting their vehicle, when really the scratch or ding was there all along.

If your coworker has a routine, like going to the gym after work, follow them there and leave the note when they're in a different parking lot. They won't suspect you, since they'll assume you went home after work.

[77]
FOR SALE

Although online marketplaces are popular for private car sales, it isn't unusual to see paper signs on vehicles as well. Hardware stores typically sell a basic template with high-visibility colors and block letters that say *For Sale*. Simply fill in your coworker's phone number in permanent marker and add a price that will make buyers want to call.

Choose a price that's low but still somewhat believable. No one is going to call about a car that's marked for $1, since that's obviously a prank or scam. Instead, make it seem like your coworker is motivated to sell and willing to take an offer on the low end.

To make this prank even better, remove the sign before your coworker goes out to the parking lot at the end of the day. They'll have no idea how prospective buyers keep getting their number. Their first instinct will be to look online when a physical sign is actually the culprit.

[78]
FRAMED!

There are plenty of joke license plate frames for sale online. Sneak out when your coworker isn't looking and add one to their vehicle. If they already have a frame, buy one in a similar color to help it blend in. Count how many days it takes for your coworker to notice that they're driving out with a car that says something embarrassing, like *Honk If You Have to Poop*.

If you don't mind spending money, consider ordering a custom frame with an inside joke or a message that's specifically tailored to your coworker. They might even decide to leave it on their car once they realize it's there.

[79]
GREEN THUMB

This prank only works if one of your coworkers drives a pickup truck with an open bed. Go to the hardware store and buy several bags of top soil. Next, grab some plastic flowers or fake plants to include in your "garden." Head back to work and arrange it all in the bed of your coworker's truck. Taller plants or flowers will have the strongest effect, since they'll stick up over the edge.

If you have time and money to spare, buy extra accessories from the gardening section to put in the parking spot around the truck. You can also sarcastically gift your coworker a watering can and gardening gloves before they see your handiwork outside.

[80]
NOT-SO-FRESH
AIR

Most air fresheners have pleasant scents that are designed to be relaxing and cozy. However, there are also prank "fresheners" with bizarre scents like pickles or poop. Sneaking one of these into your coworker's vehicle will stink up their car and leave a lingering smell that's hard to air out.

It's particularly cruel to pull this prank when you know your coworker will be spending a lot of time on the road. For example, if you know that they need to meet with a client in another location or go to a different job site, hiding a gross air freshener in their car means that they'll be stuck with it for the whole trip.

The main challenge will be accessing their vehicle without them knowing. You'll have to hope that they leave their car unlocked or come up with a convincing excuse to borrow the keys. You could also hide the air freshener in a folder and give it to them on their way out, but it won't be as effective, since it takes time for the smell to fully accumulate.

CHAPTER NINE:

SUPPLY SURPRISES

Office supplies aren't exactly exciting, which makes them the perfect items to weaponize for pranks. Your coworkers won't expect everyday objects like pens and staplers to be tools of mischief. Once they catch on to your tricks, they'll be afraid to use basic supplies without closely inspecting them for booby traps.

Unless you're willing to risk your job, it's a good idea to stick to incidental supplies that don't cost a lot of money. Your boss won't care if you damage some paper clips with your shenanigans, but they'll definitely notice if you ruin expensive calculators or burn through all the copier ink. Use your best judgment when you're raiding the supply cabinet at work.

[81]
REFILL AGAIN

Everyone goes through office supplies at their own pace, but some items are just infrequently used. Emptying your coworker's supplies and hiding the evidence will have them wondering if their memory is on the fritz. For example, you could empty their stapler once a week and only leave a few staples at the very end. Leaving the entire stapler empty would be suspicious, but if your coworker uses up the last ones, they may not catch on right away.

The same idea applies to stealing copier paper and only leaving a couple of sheets at the bottom of the tray. You could also uncap their dry-erase markers and let them mostly dry out whenever your coworker isn't around.

[82]
COPY THAT

Most people don't look at every page of their print job after they pick up copies. They just assume that the copier has clean paper that's blank on both sides. You can take advantage of their trust by sabotaging the copier with used paper.

The first step is to find something funny to scan and print. With care, you could scan a paper clip in such a way that it looks like there's a paperclip hooked over top of all subsequent copies. However, copiers are only meant for paper, so be careful about how hard you close the lid while scanning other objects. You don't want to scratch the glass or cause serious damage.

Once you've scanned a funny object or printed a joke on a few sheets, hide them in the copier's paper tray and wait for your coworkers to hit print. It's up to you to decide whether you want your additions to show up on the front or back of the paper. The front will be immediately annoying, while coworkers probably won't see anything on the back until after they walk away with their copies.

[83]
WRITING UTENSILS

Force of habit can lead to some hilarious moments. Replace your coworker's usual writing utensils with crayons and wait for them to reach over and grab one when they need to jot something down. It'll take a split second for their brain to catch up with what their eyes are seeing.

You could also purchase old-fashioned quill pens and inkwells to use as writing utensils in meetings. Ask your coworker to sign a document and hand them a quill. It'll be so unexpected that they won't know what to do.

[84]
SHARPENER
SABOTAGE

Pencil sharpeners are tough to open when it's time to empty them out. The drawers that collect shavings can't be too loose, or they'll cause a mess. Capitalize on the design by filling your coworker's pencil sharpener with glitter or confetti. When they pry the bottom out, they'll shake it everywhere and accidentally make a mess.

Test their specific pencil sharpener in advance to see how much force it takes to open. If it isn't too sticky, add a small piece of clear tape to encourage them to pull harder. When the tape tears free, it'll jar the contents and spill the glitter or confetti all over your coworker.

[85]
PEN PRANKS

Your coworker probably leaves their pens sitting out in a tray or cup. When they're away from their desk, put tiny pieces of clear tape over the ends of their pens. Their first thought will be that the pen is out of ink, but that's unlikely to happen with multiple pens in a row. They'll eventually discover the tape on the end and wonder who's responsible.

After trying to write with the pens, the tape will be mashed all around the tip. It'll take time for your coworker to remove it all. By the time they restore their pens to working condition, they might not even remember what they wanted to write down in the first place!

[86]
PAPER CLIP
CHAIN

Does your coworker keep paper clips in a box or a cutout in their desk tray? If so, you can link them all into a huge chain and put them back in the container. When your coworker goes to grab a paper clip, the entire chain will come out with it. Plus, they'll need to take the time to remove each one and return them to their original configuration.

For coworkers who don't have their paper clips in containers, fold the paper clips into the shape of a clothes hanger and attach them to their filing cabinet handles or other suitable surfaces. Depending on the size, you may even be able to find tiny doll outfits to hang on them.

[87]
MARKER
SWAP

People don't always look closely at markers before writing on dry-erase boards. They assume that the right markers are already in the tray at the bottom of the board. They'll be horrified to realize that someone swapped the dry-erase markers with permanent ones and scramble to remove the ink.

Permanent marker is designed to be, well, permanent. It often survives a good scrubbing with an eraser or all-purpose cleaners. Your coworker will panic that they've ruined an expensive whiteboard. If you feel like staging a two-part prank, let them know that they can draw over the permanent marker with a dry erase marker to make it removable. However, since you already hid all the dry erase markers, they'll need to go on a hunt to find another set.

[88]
DEAR SANTA

For this prank, you'll need to find your coworker's personal stash of envelopes. Write a fake address on the back and leave the envelope unsealed. They'll go to retrieve an envelope, only to discover that it's already due to be sent to the North Pole, Narnia, or some other ridiculous destination.

If you're motivated enough to prank the entire office, this joke is easily scalable to suit a larger collection of supplies. Raid the supply closet, sneak off with a few envelopes at a time, and return them with fake recipients written on the back. Hide your envelopes in between blank ones to make it extra frustrating when a coworker grabs a few at a time.

[89]
EMPTY INK

It's rare to run out of ink in a ballpoint pen, so your coworker won't immediately assume that's the problem when their pen won't work. They'll shake it, scribble on a piece of paper, and maybe *then* check that it still has ink inside.

Once you've stolen the ink from inside your coworker's pens, you can launch a second prank by putting them back in the wrong places. Most people expect pens to have the same color ink as the plastic on the outside. Put the blue in a black pen or red in a blue pen. If you prank multiple coworkers at once, you can even swap colors between coworkers to make it even harder to restore the pens to their original condition.

[90]
CUTTING
TIES

It's a running joke that scissors in the store should never come in a container that requires scissors to open. You can apply the same idea by using zip ties to secure all your coworkers' scissors together. When they discover your handiwork, they'll ask another person to borrow their scissors and discover that you've already pranked them, too.

Think about what other tools your coworkers might use to free their scissors and hide those as well. Remove any sturdy kitchen knives, clippers, or pocket tools that you see around the office. Your coworkers will need to go on the prowl to find something sharp enough. Since zip ties are thick and nearly impossible to pull apart by hand, this prank will create an ongoing challenge if you set it up just right.

CHAPTER TEN:

MISCELLANEOUS MAYHEM

Not every prank fits neatly into a category. This chapter offers a mix of jokes and tricks to keep things unpredictable. They may also inspire you to research similar pranks or design new ones of your own.

The key is to stay creative and figure out how to fit each one into your company's culture. Think about your coworkers' habits, preferences, and pet peeves. Those are all great clues that will allow you to ruin their day with shenanigans.

Additionally, jumping from one type of prank to another will keep your coworkers guessing. If you're always targeting lunch boxes or cars in the parking lot, it'll get predictable. With a less structured approach, your coworkers will constantly be on the lookout for trouble, because anything could be a prank.

[91]
THE CAT'S MEOW

Rather than intentionally annoying your coworkers with goofy noises like fart sounds, hide a speaker somewhere in the office and play animal noises throughout the day. Find recordings of scratching or meowing to trick people into thinking there's a critter somewhere in the building. You can also leave fake animal droppings around or bits of hair from your own pets at home.

Once people are convinced that there's a "friend" in the office, spread rumors about potential sightings. Tell coworkers that you spotted a tail disappearing around the corner of a cubicle or noticed suspicious paw prints in the snow. Give it time and see how many of your peers start to report sightings of their own.

If you're decent with Photoshop, circulate fake pictures of a cat or raccoon in various places around the office. That will make your joke more believable to your peers and help the rumors spread.

[92]
OUT OF TOUCH

Modern organizations typically have multiple generations working alongside one another. Instead of using pop culture references that align with your own age, start using phrases that are associated with older or younger generations. Not only will it give your coworkers secondhand embarrassment, but it's awkward enough that they're almost guaranteed to gossip about it when you're not around.

For example, refer to a new hire as "the cat's pajamas" or a "rad dude." When someone shows you a picture of their grandchild, react by saying they're "totes adorbs." The unusual mix of terms will throw people off.

In an ideal case, they'll need to ask you for definitions for your newfangled slang or your old-fashioned sayings. When they do, pretend that it's odd for them to not know the definitions on their own. As time goes on, add increasingly bizarre references like Shakespearean insults to see if your coworkers eventually realize it's a joke.

Obviously, this prank should be reserved for internal communications only. Your clients or external stakeholders won't appreciate having to research the meaning of antiquated terms or cultural references from the 1930s.

[93]
PICTURE
SWAP

The next time your coworker isn't paying attention, take a secret picture of them. Pretend you're sending a text message or reading something on your tablet to conceal your true actions. Once you have a decent photo that shows their face, order a copy and a frame of the same size.

Bring the framed picture to work and put it on someone else's desk. When you run into the coworker in the photo, ask them why their picture is on the other person's desk. They'll be confused and maybe a little weirded out. Make sure to stage the encounter before anyone notices the frame to make sure it's still there when your coworker goes to investigate in person.

When you're choosing targets, pick people who get along reasonably well, or at least have a similar sense of humor. You don't want your coworker to get accused of harassment or an inappropriate workplace relationship over a joke.

[94]
REDECORATING WOES

Your office probably doesn't have a resident poltergeist, but that doesn't mean that you can't fill the role. Whenever you find yourself alone in an empty area, grab a few objects and move them around to new places. Put the plastic plant in someone's cubicle or leave a box of printer paper in the middle of the kitchen. Your coworkers will wonder why everything is getting shuffled and who's to blame for it.

Eventually, people will be suspicious of anything they see out in the open. Does that stapler really belong there? Did someone mean to leave the sugar dish out on the counter? The resulting paranoia will keep everyone on their toes, so you'll need to work extra hard to avoid detection.

[95]
FRESH AIR

When people are confused about something in their environment, they often look around or at the ceiling without thinking about what's underneath them. That makes the underside of furniture the perfect place to hide a smelly surprise for your coworker. The key is to find an air freshener that's strong enough to fill the space, even if it isn't hanging out in the open.

Feign ignorance if they ask you whether you notice the smell. You could also claim to sense something else that isn't there by periodically asking if anyone smells popcorn, farts, or another strong scent. Depending on your reaction, your coworker will think it's all in their head or that everyone is experiencing a similar problem.

[96]
BRING A "FRIEND"

Think ahead to the next major holidays and which ones give you an excuse to decorate. Buy the creepiest doll you can find and bring it to work under the guise of making the office more festive. For example, you might be able to find a terrifying Santa or a doll dressed in red, white, and blue.

If not, buy a regular doll and dress it up to make it look like it's a holiday decoration. While you're at it, search for any other modifications that would increase its scare factor.

Antique dolls and accessories often have a spooky feel, especially if there's damage to their faces. Avoid going too over the top, since you don't want the creepiness to look intentional.

Bring the doll to work and display it in the same place in your office or cubicle. When people comment on it, tell them it's a cherished heirloom or a special decoration that you bring out for special occasions. After a few days, start moving the doll around the office. Put it in places where people won't see it immediately upon entering the room. They'll be in for a jolt when they notice the doll staring at them from the corner.

Progressively worsen your pranks. Move the doll directly outside the bathroom stall while your coworker is inside. Hide it behind the copier with just one limb sticking out. Before long, others will join in and create a new game around the office.

[97]
CLOCK-WATCHER

Most offices still have traditional wall clocks, since employees are not always able to check the time on their personal devices. There are also undoubtedly people in your workplace who watch the clock when it's approaching the end of a meeting or the close of the general workday. Analog clocks aren't connected to the internet and don't automatically sync, so they're perfect for messing with your clock-watching coworkers.

Simply remove the clock from the wall and adjust it to be a few minutes off from the correct time. If it's too slow, people will be annoyed that everything is taking so long. If it's too fast, they'll be irritated that meetings are running long. The exception is if they're using the clock to figure out when to go home. In that case, they'll leave a little early without realizing.

[98]
PAY RAISE

The next time you have a meeting with your supervisor or manager, pretend that you found out about a major increase in pay. Excitedly tell your friend at work at a high volume to make sure others hear you. Gush about how happy you are and explain that you're planning to get a new car, take a vacation, or make an expensive purchase.

The people around you will hone in on the fact that you received a significant pay bump, even if you don't specify the amount. They'll start to wonder about what made you special enough to single out. Not only can you laugh at their grumbling, but you might also be able to trick them into asking for a raise.

In the worst-case scenario, your boss will be angry that you spread a rumor and caused an uproar at work. But if your prank works and your peers get raises, you'll be a hero around the office, even after they discover that you were pulling their leg the whole time.

[99]
TIME TRAVEL

Search around your local thrift stores or pawn shops to see if you can find extremely old computers. Buy one and any accessories, such as a wired mouse or box speakers. When your coworker isn't around, steal their current computer and replace it with the old one you brought from home. They'll come back to a cubicle that looks like it's 1995.

The downside is that you'll need to take multiple trips to sneak larger components like the monitor into the office without anyone seeing you. The parts may also be fairly expensive if they're still in working order. It all depends on their rarity, the overall condition, and whether you were able to get a deal at the store.

If you want to go above and beyond, see if there's room to hide your coworker's laptop in the old desktop case. They won't expect it to be there, so they'll waste time looking for their laptop when it's right there next to them.

[100]
FAKE FIRED

This prank works best if you're collaborating with others on an important project. When you're facing a tough deadline, it's all hands on deck. Losing a member of the group could derail everything, which is why pretending you got fired is an awful joke to play on your coworkers.

At the end of the day, look upset and start asking your coworkers if they know where to find a sturdy box. Once you have a large box, make a show of carrying it back to your area.

Pack up any personal items and clear out your desk drawers. If anyone asks you what's going on, tell them you don't want to talk about it.

On your way out, say something like, "I guess I'll see you when I see you." That's vague enough to spur rumors without actually stating that you're not going to be back the next day. Brush off any questions in person, and don't respond to your coworkers' texts.

By the following morning, they'll be panicking that you really did get fired. When you bring your belongings back to your desk, act confused about their assumptions. Pretend it's their fault for jumping to conclusions and refuse to acknowledge that you insinuated anything with your actions. If the project you're working on is critical, you can also claim that you took your belongings home to work remotely in the evening.

[101]
DUCK INVASION

It doesn't cost much to buy large packs of rubber ducks online. Order at least a hundred and hide them around the office. In addition to cabinets and desk drawers, put some in truly unbelievable locations, like behind the refrigerator or on top of loose ceiling tiles.

After you've hidden all the ducks, send out an email to your coworkers to inform them of the duck invasion. Challenge them to find the ducks throughout the building. It could take weeks or even years to locate them all if you're clever and you have a large workplace.

If you want to keep track of which ducks are still "missing," make a spreadsheet that lists all the hiding spots and use permanent marker to number each duck. This way, you'll be able to update your coworkers about how many are still outstanding. Once they're close to finding the last few ducks, buy a set in a different color and start another round.

Once you eventually decide to leave the company, give the remaining employees an update on how many ducks are left from the latest invasion. They can still text you when they find a duck to let you know that the prank lives on.

DISCLAIMER

The intent of this book is to ruin your coworker's day by playing tricks. However, it's easy to get carried away and stray too far over the line. When in doubt, stick to pranks that are clearly harmless and all in good fun.

The ideas in this book are meant to give you a starting point, but that doesn't mean they'll be a good fit for your work environment. Think about your industry and how much joking around is tolerated. If you work for a family-owned business where everyone always pranks each other, then over-the-top stunts are probably fine. In a customer-facing role or a highly regulated industry like medicine, horsing around could get you fired.

Claiming that you were just staging a prank won't necessarily be enough to get you out of trouble. High schoolers have frequently encountered this problem while carrying out senior pranks. In 2025, six students from Johnstown, Pennsylvania, were charged with felonies after breaking into their school to wrap everything in plastic. The charges were eventually dropped, but that demonstrates the potential legal consequences of taking a prank too far.

It's also important to consider how others feel about your antics. If your coworker is already on thin ice at work, playing a joke on them could be the final straw. Similarly, you never know when someone is going through a hard time in their personal life. Pay attention to their cues and be ready to back off if it's clear that your pranks aren't welcome.

If you decide to record your pranks, be clear about what you're doing. In some states, it's illegal to record others without their permission. While you might want to maintain a record of your successful pranks, your coworkers might not want to appear on video. Always double-check before you film, especially if you plan to post the videos on social media.

Lastly, don't hesitate to make amends if one of your jokes isn't well received. Apologize or offer to replace anything that's been accidentally damaged. That will ensure that your coworkers—and your boss—don't get the wrong impression. With a little responsibility and empathy, you'll live to prank another day.

CONCLUSION

Congratulations on reaching the end of *101 Ways to Secretly Ruin Your Coworker's Day*. By now, you should have a ton of ideas about how to sabotage your coworkers and keep your peers on their toes.

Hopefully, you've found at least a few pranks that will mesh well with your workplace. Feel free to modify any of the suggestions in this book to make them fit with your schedule or environment. A little creativity can take a simple joke to the next level.

Once you earn a reputation as the company prankster, you might be fortunate enough to find kindred spirits nearby. Your peers may start to trick you in return and repay you for all the headaches. When new hires arrive, warn them about the ongoing prank war and tell them to watch out.

Ultimately, the purpose of a prank is to have fun without burning any bridges. With the right approach, you'll start new traditions and show your coworkers that it's okay to break up their routines with a little chaos from time to time. No matter what you decide to do with the pranks in this book, remember not to take yourself too seriously. Enjoy!

www.ingramcontent.com/pod-product-compliance
Lightning Source LLC
Chambersburg PA
CBHW060238030426
42335CB00014B/1513